MW01491240

Dear Tej, happy 24th.

Hope you find this book as true a source of strength and inspiration as I am. Don't forget your true self. The real Tej.

Dylan

100 Maxims
of
Guidance

© Bahram Elahi 1995

Dépôt légal 3ème trimestre 1995

100 Maxims

of

Guidance

by

Ostad Elahi

Edited by Professor Bahram Elahi

ROBERT LAFFONT

Ostad Elahi

This compilation of maxims has been published
in commemoration of the Centennial of Ostad Elahi
(1895-1974).

INTRODUCTION

The maxims selected for this compilation are extracted from the books containing accounts of the lifelong experiences of Ostad Elahi, philosopher, theologian and musician. The aim is to give the reader a foretaste of the enormous breadth of the spiritual teachings of this innovative thinker.

A fundamental principle of Ostad Elahi is that he would teach his students only the lessons already practiced by himself and found to be of true spiritual and practical value. The depth and extent of his experience as well as the exactness of his enquiries were such that they resulted in practical conclusions, varied enough to suit the needs of people from all walks of life. He was always surrounded by an interesting assortment of individuals of different religions and nationalities, rich and poor, literate and illiterate, villagers, business people, students, scholars, musicians, etc. Answers to theoretical questions were often accompanied by practical solutions and tangible examples commonly encountered in daily life. Everyone benefited from his lessons, each according to their own capacity or heart-felt enthusiasm, all enjoying easy and friendly relations with him. The atheist who came for a debate, the musician who sought his advice on some musical technicality, the scholar who wished to widen the scope of his research, the spiritual traveller who sought salvation for his soul and the sick person who sought relief from physical pain — Ostad welcomed them all with his characteristic gentle smile and always had time to deal with all their varied problems.

It is hoped that the reader will find warmth and guidance in these maxims and take them as a brief introduction to the universal teachings of Ostad Elahi.

Bahram Elahi

OSTAD ELAHI   (1895-1974)

Ostad Elahi was born on September 11, 1895, in Jeyhunabad, a small village in Western Iran. His father, Haj Ne'mat, was a prolific writer and mystical poet who was recognized as a saint. From childhood on, Ostad Elahi led an ascetic, secluded life of rigorous spiritual discipline under his father's watchful supervision. He received the classical education of that time, with a special focus on religion and ethics.

At the age of twenty-four he left his spiritual retreat, breaking with the local tradition that would have destined him to an entirely contemplative life. He moved to Tehran, where he worked in the Registry Office and began to study Civil Law. This radical change in his life, he later explained, was necessary for him to deepen his thinking and to test his ethical and religious principles in the face of the demands of an ordinary life in society. In 1933, he successfully completed his studies at the Superior School of Jurisprudence. For nearly 30 years he was appointed to positions of increasing responsibility throughout the country, sometimes as Public Prosecutor and at other times as Examining Magistrate. He eventually became an Associate Justice and then the Chief Justice of the National Court of Appeals.

Throughout this period of his work as a judge, Ostad Elahi continued to devote a great deal of time to his personal studies and research, especially in the areas of philosophy and theology. Although little is known about the unfolding course of his thought during those years, it is clear that this period was filled with experiences that richly nourished his esoteric studies and helped him formulate his later teachings. At the same time, spiritual music, which he had pursued since early childhood, continued to hold an important place in his life. He was acknowledged by musical specialists to be a great virtuoso of the *tanbur* (a kind of lute), enriching its repertoire through many original musical compositions.

Ostad Elahi retired from the judiciary in 1957, and only then did he really begin to reveal his own way of thought. He wrote two major scholarly works on religion and spirituality, in addition to an extensive commentary on one of his father's writings . The practical spiritual aspect of Ostad Elahi's thought was more fully developed in the oral teaching and instruction that he relayed to a few friends and students until the end of his life in 1974. Two extensive volumes of his sayings and teachings have been published to date on the basis of notes written down by his students.

Ostad Elahi's work defines a rigorous practical method that can be used to answer the eternal questions about our nature as human beings, our place in the universe and our ultimate destination. His work demonstrates the possibility of reasserting the fundamental importance of our spiritual dimension. Ostad Elahi's thought sheds new light on the concept of religion. He defines Religion as the quintessence of all the revealed religions and presents it as a collection of objective, systematic and experimental forms of understanding that can best be called a "science". It thus becomes universal — independent of any particular ritual, history or culture. This approach does not deny the legitimacy of each religion, rather it stresses that their differences are only external and secondary. The essential, universal dimension of religion is the means by which we human beings can fulfill our primordial nature and complete our metaphysical destiny. This process of spiritual perfection is the fundamental theme of Ostad Elahi's teachings.

Human fulfillment requires something more than mere philosophical reflection. Religion, like any science, must necessarily be grounded in verifiable experiences. What Ostad Elahi passed on, in his written and oral teachings, is the direct result of such experiences and not mere philosophical theory. Ostad Elahi's thought provides a practical, ethical foundation for the accomplishment of our intrisic human duties. The first of those duties is to understand the true dimensions of our Self, not just in theory but also in practice. This Self-understanding comes about through our striving to reach the right harmony and balance between the material and spiritual dimensions existent in each human being. The unique quality of his thought is that it presents a method by which a student can practice spiritual principles and derive results that confirm their truth. This dynamic process leads the individual seeker into a confrontation with his or her own Self in the context of ongoing interaction with society.

On the Path of Truth, there is no distinction between religions, races, man and woman.

The mainspring of knowledge is to realise why we have been brought into existence, what our duties are as human beings, and what our final goal is.

Esoteric knowledge is the fruit of esoteric practice and the ultimate goal of philosophy and wisdom.

When you come to realise that all the saints and prophets are legitimate, and you no longer make a distinction between religions, then you will reach the stage of true spiritual understanding.

Only that which is durable and permanent deserves to be the object of our attention, for things of this world are perishable, and this is certain; riches, youth, honour, and all the pleasures of this life are ephemeral.

Attention to God is the highest form of prayer.

Respecting the rights of others is the keystone to the edifice of life in this world.

How noble it is to help someone, be wronged by him in return, and yet forgive him.

To find God, look into your heart. Then you'll see that God is everywhere and that there is nothing but Him.

To feel compassionate even towards one's enemies is a sign of nobleness and spiritual perfection.

Sow the seeds in this world and reap the harvest in the next. Take care to sow well and you will have a good harvest.

On the Path of Perfection selfishness, self-centredness, and self-satisfaction are among the worst defects.

To do all we can to serve society is the true meaning of piety, altruism, and love of God.

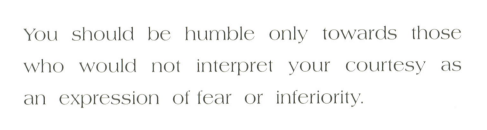

You should be humble only towards those who would not interpret your courtesy as an expression of fear or inferiority.

The best pleasure is to do without the pleasures of the imperious self.

Those who are both knowledgeable and wise are very useful to society.

When you look deep within yourself, everything will become clear.

Walking the Path of God may be summed up in two principles: turning one's attention towards the Creator and serving others.

A true traveller on the path of God is one who observes the social and moral rules as well as the civil and religious laws.

What makes creatures different from one another is the degree of their proximity to the Necessary Being as well as certain factors resulting from the Divine Wisdom.

A traveller on the Path must avoid everything that causes addiction or distraction.

Will-power is the key that gives access to all spiritual levels.

A human being worthy of this name rejoices in the happiness of others and sympathises with them in their sorrows.

See nothing as bad; never speak ill of anything or anyone; and do not look down upon any creature.

God loves those who spare no efforts when trying to achieve something and, at the same time, rely inwardly on Him.

Acquiring moral qualities requires spiritual aptitude and does not depend solely upon education.

Do not put your hope in anyone but God.

To strengthen will-power natural aptitude is necessary, but practice and self-suggestion are also very useful.

To succeed in material things we must be organised and active; it is the same with spiritual matters.

Intention rooted in goodness and kindness will, by itself, bear fruit.

Jealousy first corrodes the heart and then reaches out for others.

True happiness is to have in one's possession the means of ensuring one's salvation and spiritual destiny on the Path of Perfection.

It is impossible for those who have pure and sincere faith not to be respected in society and not to succeed in their affairs.

When praying, the essential thing is to have one's attention so focused on the Divine Presence as to feel that one is not alone.

Words rooted in personal experience and observation have great impact.

A true spiritual traveller must not feel hurt by, nor complain about, the behaviour of others.

The closer to dawn the night prayer gets, the more it gains in worth and value.

It is everyone's duty to be useful in society.

Right and Truth will always prevail, provided we remain steadfast in our convictions and make sure to put them into practice.

Anger is like a deadly poison to the soul. The more it decreases, the more the soul's positive magnetic force increases.

To find inner peace, one should not be overly concerned with such things as unemployment, poverty, death, etc.

As long as man has an ego, he cannot love God. For God to come, the ego must go.

L'ESSENTIEL EST LA LIAISON DU CŒUR AVEC LA SOURCE.

Look into yourself to find the reason for everything that happens to you.

Love is the root of all. If the root rots then everything you have decays.

Nothing is better for a spiritual traveller than keeping the goal constantly in mind.

For your prayers and acts of devotion ask for no recompense except God's satisfaction.

Dignity belongs to those who live contentedly, and wretched are those whose greed knows no bounds.

Allowing oneself to be swindled is to be unjust to those who are truly needy.

The broader the mind, the greater the tolerance.

The following religious prescriptions are particularly precious and useful in this world and the next :

To have our attention always turned towards the Almighty.

To be always conscious that He is omnipresent and omniscient.

To comply with everything prescribed by Him.

To avoid everything proscribed by Him.

To treat others with kindness, honesty and goodwill.

Those who know about Spiritual Truth and have the power to defend it have the duty to make it known to others. Failure to do this is a kind of spiritual treason.

We should ask God for nothing but His satisfaction.

Overcoming the imperious self is better than doing good deeds, for without dominating the imperious self, one may lose the spiritual benefits of good deeds already accomplished.

A human being worthy of this name distinguishes himself by his compassion, generosity and goodwill.

Pride is so harmful that, more than any other sin, it weakens the soul and strengthens the imperious self.

We must dedicate our heart to God, our hands to good deeds and the service of others, and our tongue to good words.

Man is responsible for his actions in so far as God has given him will-power, discernment, and free-will. Beyond this, his future is determined by God.

A pure heart shelters love and light, not malice and darkness.

Sincere acts, accomplished only for God's satisfaction, have lasting effects that never become stale.

DIEU · EST · LA · LUMIERE · DES · CIELS · ET · DE · LA · TERRE · SA · LUMIERE · EST · PAREILLE · A · UNE · NICHE · AVEC · UNE LAMPE

UNE LAMPE · ... EST RE ET ... ME UN ... TOUCHE · FEU LA · LUMIERE · ET LUMI ... DU CRISTAL · DU CRISTAL · DANS EST · ORIENT · NI D' · NI D'OCCI · OLIVIER · QUI · A UN ARBRE BENI · ELLE EST · ALLUME · ET · L'HUI · D'OCCI · ECLAIRERAIT · SANS · QUE · LE · FEU · LA · TOUCHE

ALLUME · ELE · ECLAIR

One who raises a child well
can govern a country.

If we succeed in looking deep within ourselves, concentrating our attention, we can solve the insoluble, for God has given us all the power to do so.

The necessary condition for looking within oneself is never to feel alone. Whether by yourself or with others, awake or asleep, in motion or at rest, you should always feel yourself in the presence of God, for He is always present, watching over your thoughts and actions.

Where one is buried is of little importance; what is important and what counts in the next world is the good deeds we have accomplished in this world.

The soul is so sensitive that the torment it feels when reprimanded in the spiritual world is much more intense than any physical suffering experienced in this world.

Those who pardon while having the power to avenge themselves shall receive spiritual honours.

The soul is totally devoid of pride and arrogance. Whenever you detect pride in yourself, be certain that it comes from the imperious self.

On your spiritual journey, do not let temptation, doubt, or pride get hold of you in any way, for on the Path of Perfection there are no greater dangers.

Chance does not exist. There is always a cause and a reason for everything.

The one who says "I know" is more ignorant than the ignorant. One must always learn from others.

Peace and order in society rest on three pillars: religious laws, social laws and moral laws.

Defects, such as anger, jealousy, greed and lying, are signs of imperfection and are obstacles to the awakening of the spiritual senses. One who wants to travel the Path of Perfection must struggle against these defects, which are part of human nature.

While praying, you must imagine that you are talking to someone. In conversation, you would not utter a word without knowing its meaning. Similarly, when praying, you should understand the meaning of each word and know to whom you are speaking and what your are saying.

To be created, to be brought from non-existence into being, is a grace bestowed upon us by the Creator.

reste que Lui

To the extent that God has given us the power and freedom to act, we have the duty to make use of our thought, will-power and perseverance. If despite all our efforts we make no progress, we should know that it all comes from elsewhere.

We must make a habit of struggling against our defects until this becomes our second nature.

Try always to secure what is rightfully yours, rather than inspiring pity.

In everything, progress is made through regular training and exercise; it is the same in spirituality.

The Creator is the One Who surpasses the limits of our understanding.

To lose hope in Divine Clemency is one of the greatest sins.

If used for spiritual purposes, music will connect us to the divine, for music is related to the soul and the soul is related to God. Pity it has been turned into a vehicle solely for material enjoyment.

Of all the branches of knowledge, those useful for society are those that also have a positive spiritual effect.

God has entrusted man with life, maturity, will-power, reason, knowledge, dignity, social position, virtue, and piety. To fail in one's duty towards any of them is treason.

Every creature is endowed
with a certain potential
which can be developed,
but not exceeded.

To neglect one's health is to betray life; to be capricious is to betray maturity; to lack perseverance is to betray will-power; to act on impulse is to betray reason; to act with baseness is to betray dignity; to remain ignorant is to betray knowledge; to misuse power is to betray social position; to succumb to debauchery is to betray virtue; blasphemy is a betrayal of piety.

The shadow of nostalgia, longing, regret, remorse, bitter memories and fear of death is cast over mankind. No one escapes it except those who engage in spiritual practice.

Each step taken by way of renouncing the desires of the imperious self is a step taken in the direction of satisfying the longings of the soul, and this is what brings us closer to the Creator.

The forces of attraction exercised on the earth and on the creatures, all derive from the force of Divine attraction.

You must reach the point where you find praying a joy and a pleasure, not an obligation.

Prayer must not be reduced to a mere repetition of formulas; rather, it must be a combination of action, concentration and contemplation.

One must first develop a dignified character, and then attend to the education of the soul.

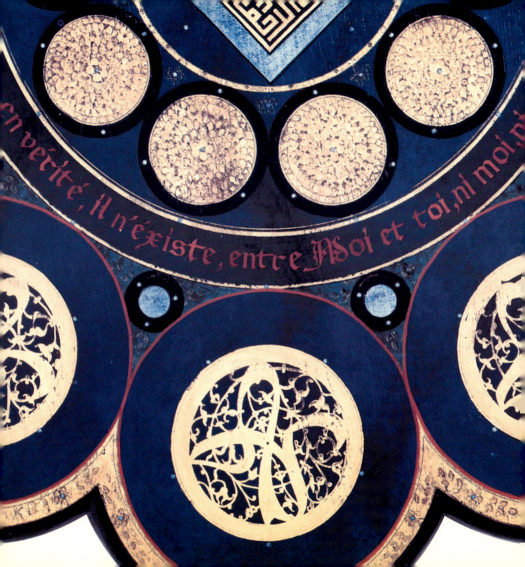

The precept of successive lives is the key to the process of perfecting the soul.

In society you must always conduct yourself with propriety, modesty, and courtesy.

The more we expand and deepen our knowledge, the more we become conscious of our own insignificance and of the immensity of God.

It is possible to imagine paradise, but Perfection is beyond all imagination.

Divine commandments are all founded on one principle : respecting the rights of others.

Be confident that God exists, and that there is a world beyond this one — the world of souls.

Music has countless properties, most of which are not yet discovered.

Anyone who knows and observes the authentic commandments of his religion with faith shall reach the Truth.

In the hearts of some people there are particles that radiate like the sun, though these people have an ordinary appearance.

No force can hinder the development and diffusion of that which bears the stamp of God.

Further reading on the life and teachings of Ostad Elahi:

- *Words of Faith: Prayers by Ostad Elahi*,
  Robert Laffont. France 1995.

- *Unicity: A Collection of Photographs
  of Ostad Elahi*,
  Robert Laffont. France 1995.

- *The Path of Perfection* by Bahram Elahi,
  Element books Ltd. Great Britain 1993.

- *The Way of Light* by Bahram Elahi,
  Element books Ltd. Great Britain 1993.

The illustrations in this book have been made from details of the paintings entitled «Polylobes» by André Marzuk, as well as from a collage series of «Polylobes» entitled «Quarante-deux louanges au Regard».

© Spadem 1995

Printed by Toscane Press in Nice, France, 1995